How to . . .

get the most from your
COLES NOTES

Key Point

Basic concepts in point form.

Close Up

Additional hints, notes, tips or background information.

Watch Out!

Areas where problems frequently occur.

Quick Tip

Concise ideas to help you learn what you need to know.

Remember This!

Essential material for mastery of the topic.

COLES NOTES

Getting Along in ...

Japanese

For travellers &

merchants

Useful phrases with

pronunciations

Travel & culture tips

COLES NOTES have been an indispensable aid to students on five continents since 1948.

COLES NOTES now offer titles on a wide range of general interest topics as well as traditional academic subject areas and individual literary works. All COLES NOTES are written by experts in their fields and reviewed for accuracy by independent authorities and the Coles Editorial Board.

COLES NOTES provide clear, concise explanations of their subject areas. Proper use of COLES NOTES will result in a broader understanding of the topic being studied. For academic subjects, COLES NOTES are an invaluable aid for study, review and exam preparation. For literary works, COLES NOTES provide interesting interpretations and evaluations which supplement the text but are not intended as a substitute for reading the text itself. Use of the NOTES will serve not only to clarify the material being studied, but should enhance the reader's enjoyment of the topic.

© Copyright 1999 and Published by
COLES PUBLISHING. A division of Prospero Books.
Toronto – Canada
Printed in Canada

Cataloguing in Publication Data
Kitagawa, Randy, 1967–
Getting along in — Japanese

(Coles notes)
Written by Randy Kitagawa and Mina Kitagawa.
ISBN 0-7740-0628-5

1. Japanese language – Conversation and phrase books – English.
I. Kitagawa, Mina, 1965–. II. Title. III. Series.

PL539.K53 1999   495.6'83421   C99-932454-3

Publisher: Nigel Berrisford
Editor: Paul Kropp Communications
Writers: Randy Kitagawa, Mina Kitagawa
Book design: Karen Petherick
Layout: Richard Hunt

Printed and bound in Canada by Webcom Limited
Cover finish: Webcom's Exclusive DURACOAT

Contents

Japanese in a nutshell

Here is a list of very common Japanese expressions well worth memorizing on your flight over. The Japanese writing in this book will help if you have difficulty with some words or phases. Have the person simply read the expression for those tough ones.

Good morning.	Ohayoo gozaimasu.	おはようございます。
Good afternoon.	Konnichiwa.	こんにちは。
Good evening.	Konbanwa.	こんばんは。
Goodbye.	Sayoonara.	さようなら。
Yes/No.	Hai/Iie.	はい/いいえ。
Okay.	Ookee.	オーケー。
Please (when speaker is offering something).	Doozo.	どうぞ。
Please (when speaker is requesting something).	Onegai shimasu.	お願いします。
Do you have...	...arimasu ka?	...ありますか？
Thank you.	Arigatoo.	ありがとう。
You're welcome.	Dooitashimashite.	どういたしまして。
Excuse me.	Sumimasen.	すみません。
I understand.	Wakarimashita.	わかりました。

I don't understand.	Wakarimasen.	わかりません。
Do you speak English?	Eigo o hanashimasu ka?	英語を話しますか？
I'm Canadian.	Watashi wa Kanadajin desu.	私はカナダ人です。
How much is it?	Ikura desu ka?	いくらですか？

Welcome to *Getting Along in Japanese*. This phrase book and guide is full of very useful phases for new students of the Japanese language or those travelling to Japan on business or vacation. The chapters have been divided into sections that most travelers will encounter during a visit. A special section has been included for those who serve Japanese tourists in Canada. All chapters have a short introduction as well as tips and notes on issues related to the topic. Take the time to go over the pronunciation section in this book. If you have difficulty pronouncing some words or phrases, take advantage of the Japanese writing that is included in this book by pointing at the expression that you wish to convey.

As you'll learn on your trip, Japan has a population of 123 million people and consists of four main islands, Honshu, Shikoku, Kyushu and Hokkaido. With 80 percent of its region mountainous, the majority of people live in and around urban centers. The crowds can be overwhelming – so when travelling in the city try to use public transportation during off peak times whenever possible. Have a good trip!

CHAPTER ONE

A pronunciation guide

The pronunciation system used in this guide is basically the system used in most Japanese-English dictionaries. As in speaking any language, correct pronunciation is essential to make yourself understood. The spelling system used in this book is designed to enable you to communicate in Japanese in the shortest time. Japanese pronunciation is quite simple for native English speakers. There are only 24 basic sounds. Once you have mastered the five vowel sounds, you will have no problem with pronouncing Japanese words. Japanese is a syllabic language with all but one of its basic syllables ending with one of the five vowel sounds. Syllables are composed of the following elements. Each element is distinctly pronounced with equal duration:

- basic vowel sounds a i u e o
- consonant(s) + vowel(s) (e.g., ta, ni, fu, etc.) and modified consonant vowel combinations (e.g., ga)
- n
- combined sounds (e.g., kya, shya, cha, etc.)

Japanese writing is made up of pictographic characters adopted from the Chinese language, phonetic symbols or a combination of both. Called *kana* these phonetic symbols are divided into two types, *hiragana* and *katakana*. Each symbol represents the sound of one syllable. The alphabet is used in this book to simplify things.

Basic vowel sounds

The letters a, i, u, e, o represent the five basic vowel sounds in Japanese. They are pronounced as follows:

a   as in father

i   as in eat

u   as in fruit

e   as in met

o   as in go

Vowels will be doubled to show twice the length of the sound as a single short vowel. So when you see a double vowel, pronounce it in the same way as a single vowel for double the amount of time.

Long vowels are indicated as follows:

aa

ii

uu

ee

oo

Combined vowel sounds

The vowel sounds can be combined with different consonants and consonant combinations to make up the rest of the Japanese phonetic alphabet.

Here is a list of all basic consonant vowel combinations in the Japanese language.

ka   ki   ku   ke   ko
(the k sound is pronounced as in kite)

sa   shi   su   se   so
(the s sound is pronounced as in sad)

ta   chi   tsu   te   to
(the t sound is pronounced as in toe)

na   ni   nu   ne   no
(the n sound is pronounced as in nice)

ha   hi   hu (fu) he   ho
(the h sound is pronounced as in ham)

ma   mi   mu   me   mo
(the m sound is pronounced as in mother)

ya   yu   yo
(the y sound is pronounced as in yes)

ra   ri   ru   re   ro
See the box below.

wa
(the w sound is pronounced as in what)

n
(the n sound is pronounced with your mouth closed as in the name Ann)

R in Japanese

The r sound is perhaps the most difficult to pronounce. The Japanese r sound is pronounced more like an L in English – for example, pronounce "ramen" (Japanese noodle) with an L…lamen.

Modified consonant and vowel combinations include:

ga   gi   gu   ge   go
(the g sound is pronounced as in garden)

za   ji   zu   ze   zo
(the z sound is pronounced as in zoom, the j sound is pronounced as in jeans)

da   ji   zu   de   do
(the d sound is pronounced as in dad)

ba   bi   bu   be   bo
(the b sound is pronounced as in bob)

pa   pi   pu   pe   po
(the p sound is pronounced as in push)

Syllabic "n" sound

The consonant n can be a syllable by itself when it comes before another consonant or at the end of a word. In a few cases, when it precedes a vowel, it is pronounced on its own as a single syllable.

e.g., Konnichiwa: The first n is pronounced as its own syllable. The second n is combined with the next vowel and is pronounced as ni: ko-n-ni-chi-wa

Modified syllables

The final sounds that can be found in the Japanese language are modified syllables that are combined with other syllables to form words:

kya	kyu	kyo
sha	shu	sho
cha	chu	cho
nya	nyu	nyo
hya	hyu	hyo
mya	myu	myo
rya	ryu	ryo
gya	gyu	gyo
jya	jyu	jyo
bya	byu	byo
pya	pyu	pyo

Double consonants

The double consonant is also common in many words. They are kk, pp, ss, tt and tch. Before a double consonant, there is a slight pause at the first consonant, then you continue with a stress on the second consonant. You take a short breath before you pronounce the second consonant. For example, *kip pu* – ticket or *kit te* – stamp.

Borrowed words

Like many languages, Japanese has incorporated many foreign words. Some of these words, especially Chinese and Korean elements, have been an integral part of the native language for thousands of years. Certain Dutch and Portuguese terms were introduced just a few hundred years ago. You will find borrowed words a very useful and easy way to expand your basic Japanese vocabulary. However, you should take care to pronounce each syllable clearly in order to be understood.

Here are a few examples of common words used in Japanese that have been taken from other languages:

hoteru – hotel

pan - bread (Portuguese)

furaido poteto – french fries

hotto koohii – hot coffee

koora – Coke

kamera – camera

sutereo – stereo

terebi – television

suutsu keesu – suitcase

arigato – thank you
(from the Portuguese
"thank you")

arubaito – part time job
(from the German "work")

SIGNS YOU WILL SEE

出口	deguchi	exit
入口	iriguchi	entrance
非常口	hijoguchi	emergency exit
押す	osu	push (door)
引く	hiku	pull (door)
止まる	tomaru	stop
開く	hiraku	open (elevator)
閉る	shimaru	close (elevator)
中央口	chuuooguchi	central entrance/exit
東口	higashi guchi	east entrance/exit
西口	nishi guchi	west entrance/exit
南口	minami guchi	south entrance/exit
北口	kita guchi	north entrance/exit
駅	eki	train station
地下鉄	chikatetsu	subway
切符売り場	kippuuriba	ticket vending machine
精算所	seisanjo	fare adjustment machine
新幹線	shinkansen	bullet train
お手洗い	otearai	toilet
洗面所	senmenjo	washroom
男子用（紳士）	danshiyoo (shinshi)	men's washroom

女子用（婦人）	joshiyoo(fujin)	ladies washroom
タクシー乗り場	takushiinoriba	taxi stop
バス停	basutei	bus stop
公衆電話	kooshyu denwa	public telephone
交番	kooban	police station
案内所	annaijo	information
危険	kiken	danger
立入禁止	tachiirikinshi	keep out

Japanese writing is made up of phonetic symbols, hiragana and katakana (listed below) and pictographic characters or *kanji*. The chart will help you read words not included in this book.

HIRAGANA & KATAKANA CHART

a あ ア	i い イ	u う ウ	e え エ	o お オ
ka か カ	ki き キ	ku く ク	ke け ケ	ko こ コ
sa さ サ	shi し シ	su す ス	se せ セ	so そ ソ
ta た タ	chi ち チ	tsu つ ツ	te て テ	to と ト
na な ナ	ni に ニ	nu ぬ ヌ	ne ね ネ	no の ノ
ha は ハ	hi ひ ヒ	fu ふ フ	he へ ヘ	ho ほ ホ
ma ま マ	mi み ミ	mu む ム	me め メ	mo も モ
ya や ヤ		yu ゆ ユ		yo よ ヨ
ra ら ラ	ri り リ	re る ル	re れ レ	ro ろ ロ
wa わ ワ				o を ヲ

CHAPTER TWO

The basics

For the most part, this book covers speech at a formal level. Formal speech is used with travellers and other unfamiliar persons in everyday situations or in a business setting. Informal speech is only used among friends and family.

"Aisatsu" means "greeting" in Japanese – and it is a very important part of the Japanese culture. Take the time to go over and practice the following greetings. Please remember – you can never be too polite in Japan.

GREETINGS

Good morning.	Ohayoo gozaimasu.	おはようございます。
Good afternoon.	Konnichiwa.	こんにちは。
Good evening.	Konbanwa.	こんばんは。
Good night.	Oyasuminasai.	おやすみなさい。
See you later.	Mata atode.	また あとで。
Goodbye.	Sayoonara.	さようなら。
Take care.	Kiotsukete.	気をつけて。
Long time no see.	Hisashiburi.	久しぶり。

INTRODUCTIONS

It is not customary to shake hands when meeting someone for the first time. A friendly smile and bow is how most Japanese people greet each other.

When addressing people other than family members, always remember to use the suffix *san* after their name. The suffix *san* is a sign of respect and is never used when you are referring to yourself.

For example, When addressing Mrs. Mina Tanaka, you would say Tanaka-san or Mr. Toshi Sakai would be Sakai-san. First names are only used with close friends and family.

My name is…	Watashi no namae wa…desu.	わたしの名前は…. です。
What is your name?	Anata no namae wa nan desu ka ?	あなたの名前は なんですか？
Nice to meet you.	Hajimemashite.	はじめまして。
How are you?	Ogenki desu ka ?	お元気ですか？
Fine thank you. And you?	Watashi wa genki desu. Anata wa?	私は元気です。 あなたは？
Not bad, thanks.	Maamaa desu.	まあまあです。

GENERAL EXPRESSIONS

When you are asking for something, use "onegai shimasu," which means please. For example "Okanjo onegai shimasu!" May I have the cheque please! Or "kudasai" can also be used to say the same thing. Okanjo kudasai! Cheque please!

Please (when speaker is requesting something).	Onegai shimasu.	お願いします。
Please (when speaker is requesting something)	Kudasai.	ください。
Please (when offering something).	Doozo.	どうぞ。
Do you have…?	…arimasu ka?	…ありますか？
Yes.	Hai.	はい。
No.	Iie.	いいえ。
Thank you.	Arigatoo.	ありがとう。
No thank you.	Iie, kekkoo desu.	いいえ、結構です。
Okay.	Ookee.	オーケー。
I'm sorry.	Gomennasai.	ごめんなさい。
Excuse me.	Sumimasen.	すみません。
You're welcome.	Dooitashimashite.	どういたしまして。
Please wait a moment.	Chotto matte kudasai.	ちょっと待って ください。
No problem.	Daijobu desu.	大丈夫です。
How much is it?	Ikura desu ka?	いくらですか？

What time is it?	Nanji desu ka ?	何時 ですか？
Where is the washroom?	Toire wa doko desu ka?	トイレはどこ ですか？
I don't understand.	Wakarimasen.	わかりません。
Please speak slowly.	Yukkuri hanashite kudasai	ゆっくり話して ください。
Please repeat that.	Mooichido itte kudasai.	もう一度言って ください。
Please write it down.	Kaite kudasai.	書いて下さい。
Let's go.	Ikimashyo.	行きましょう。
Is it okay?	Ii desu ka ?	いいですか？

Sounds you may hear at the end of the sentence.

In many cases, one sound at the end of the sentence can change the meaning of the entire expression.

ka - indicates a question.
ne - indicates the speaker is seeking agreement, similar to our Canadian eh.
yo - is used to emphasize a point.

For example, Onaka ga suite imasu. I'm hungry.
  Onaka ga suite imasu ka? Are you hungry?

QUESTION WORDS

Who?	Dare?	だれ？
Where?	Doko?	どこ？
What?	Nani?	なに？
Why?	Naze?	なぜ？
When?	Itsu?	いつ？
How?	Donoyooni?	どのように？
How many?	Ikutsu?	いくつ？
How much?	Ikura?	いくら？

NUMBERS

1	ichi	一
2	ni	二
3	san	三
4	shi or yon	四
5	go	五
6	roku	六
7	shichi or nana	七
8	hachi	八
9	ku or kyu	九
10	juu	十
11	juu ichi	十一
20	nijuu	二十
21	nijuu-ichi	二十一
30	sanjuu	三十
40	yonjuu	四十
50	gojuu	五十

100	hyaku	百
101	hyaku ichi	百一
200	ni hyaku	二百
300	san byaku	三百
400	yon hyaku	四百
500	go hyaku	五百
600	rop pyaku	六百
700	nana hyaku	七百
800	hap pyaku	八百
900	kyuu hyaku	九百
1,000	sen	千
2,000	ni sen	二千
10,000	ichi man	一万

Counters – Used with inanimate objects only

one	hitotsu	1つ
two	futatsu	2つ
three	mittsu	3つ
four	yottsu	4つ
five	itsutsu	5つ
six	muttsu	6つ
seven	nanatsu	7つ
eight	yattsu	8つ
nine	kokonotsu	9つ
ten	jukko	10個

DAYS OF THE WEEK

Today is ...	*Kyoo wa ...*	今日は...
Monday	Getsuyoobi	月曜日
Tuesday	Kayoobi	火曜日
Wednesday	Suiyoobi	水曜日
Thursday	Mokuyoobi	木曜日
Friday	Kinyoobi	金曜日
Saturday	Doyoobi	土曜日
Sunday	Nichiyoobi	日曜日
tomorrow	ashita (asu)	明日
yesterday	kinoo	昨日

MONTHS AND DATES

January 1	Ichi gatsu tsuitachi	1月1日
February 2	Ni gatsu futsuka	2月2日
March 3	San gatsu mikka	3月3日
April 4	Shi gatsu yokka	4月4日
May 5	Go gatsu itsuka	5月5日
June 6	Roku gatsu muika	6月6日
July 7	Shichi gatsu nanoka	7月7日
August 8	Hachi gatsu yooka	8月8日
September 9	Ku gatsu kokonoka	9月9日
October 10	Juu gatsu tooka	10月10日
November 15	Juu ichi gatsu juu go nichi	11月15日
December 30	Juu ni gatsu san juu nichi	12月30日

SEASONS

spring	haru	春
summer	natsu	夏
fall	aki	秋
winter	fuyu	冬

DIRECTION

north	kita	北
south	minami	南
east	higashi	東
west	nishi	西
right	migi	右
left	hidari	左
straight	massugu	まっすぐ

TIME

morning	gozen	午前
afternoon	gogo	午後
evening	yuugata	夕方
night	yoru	夜
1 o'clock	ichi-ji	1時
2 o'clock	ni-ji	2時
3 o'clock	san-ji	3時
4 o'clock	yo-ji	4時
5 o'clock	go-ji	5時
6 o'clock	roku-ji	6時
7 o'clock	shichi-ji	7時
8 o'clock	hachi-ji	8時

9 o'clock	ku-ji	9時
10 o'clock	juu-ji	10時
11 o'clock	juuichi-ji	11時
12 o'clock	juuni-ji	12時
12:30	juuni-ji han	12時半

SAMPLE PHRASES

I will be arriving on Friday, June 25.

Watashi wa roku-gatsu nijuugo-nichi no kinyoobi ni toochaku shimasu.

私は6月25日の金曜日に到着します。

I will be arriving at 9:00 am.

Watashi wa gozen ku-ji ni tsukimasu.

私は午前9時に着きます。

I will be leaving on Monday, July 5.

Watashi wa shichi-gatsu itsuka no getsuyoobi ni shyuppatsu shimasu

私は7月5日の月曜日に出発します。

Please meet me on Tuesday, August 10 at 2:00 pm.

Hachi-gatsu tooka kayoobi no gogo ni-ji ni atte kudasai.

8月10日火曜日の午後2時に会ってください。

I want to go to Kyoto on September 22.

Ku-gatsu nijuuninichi ni kyooto e ikitai desu.

9月22日に京都へ行きたいです。

16

Do you have a room available on Thursday, May 31.

Go-gatsu sanjuuichi-nichi mokuyoobi ni heya wa aiteimasu ka?

5月31日木曜日に部屋は空いていますか？

I would like to make a reservation on Saturday, March 11.

Go-gatsu juuichi-nichi no doyoobi ni yoyaku o onegaishimasu.

3月11日の土曜日に予約をお願します。

CHAPTER THREE

Upon arrival

All visitors entering Japan, regardless of your visa or length of stay, will be asked to fill out a registration card. Be sure to fill out all the pertinent information in order to avoid delays at customs and immigration.

You will be able to get by at the airport speaking English. In the city however, try asking students when you need help. Students take mandatory English courses in school and therefore will more likely be able to help you. English is Japan's second language.

Here is my ...	Kore ga watashi no ... desu	これが私の ...です。
passport	pasupooto	パスポート
visa	biza	ビザ
I am on vacation.	Watashi wa kankoo de kimashita.	私は観光で来ました。
I am here on business.	Watashi wa shigoto de kimashita.	私は仕事で来ました。
I am going to be here for ...	*Watashi wa kokoni ... taizai shimasu.*	私はここに...滞在します。
2 days	futsuka	2日
1 week	isshyukan	1週間

2 weeks	nishyukan	2週間
1 month	ikkagetsu	1ヶ月
I am just passing through.	Norikae dake desu.	乗り換えだけです。
I am travelling ...	*Watashi wa ... ryokoo shite imasu.*	私は...旅行しています。
alone	hitori de	一人で
with my colleague	dooryoo to	同僚と
with my wife	tsuma to	妻と
with my husband	shyujin to	主人と
with my friend	tomodachi to	友達と
with my family	kazoku to	家族と
I am staying at the ... hotel.	Watashi wa ... hoteru ni taizai shimasu.	私は...ホテルに滞在します。
I am staying in (Tokyo).	Watashi wa (Tokyo) ni taizai shimasu.	私は東京に滞在します。

AT CUSTOMS

I have nothing to declare.	Shinkoku suru mono wa arimasen.	申告するものはありません。
I have some gifts for friends.	Tomodachi ni omiyage ga arimasu.	友達におみやげがあります。
I want to declare ...	*Watashi wa ... o shinkoku shimasu.*	私は...を申告します。
this camera	kono kamera	このカメラ
this computer	kono konpuutaa	このコンピューター

Where is...?	...wa doko desu ka?	...は どこですか？
the baggage claim	Tenimotsu hikitorijo	手荷物引き取り所
the tourist information desk	Kankoo annaijo	観光案内所
the money exchange desk	Ryoogaejo	両替所
a telephone	Denwa	電話
a taxi stand	Takushii noriba	タクシー乗り場
the limousine bus stand	Rimujin basu noriba	リムジンバス乗り場
I am missing a suitcase.	Suutsu keesu ga dete kimasen.	スーツケースが 出てきません。

GETTING INTO TOWN

Before making your way to your final destination, make sure that you have enough cash for a few days. Although credit cards are becoming more popular, many restaurants, shops and cheaper accommodations still do not accept them.

There are a number of ways that you can get into town. Most visitors will use the train or bus service since driving is difficult and expensive. Bus service drops passengers off at major hotels and train stations in the city. Both services run on regular schedules; however, if you're taking the bus take into consideration the time you may spend in traffic. Most seats on buses departing from the airport are reserved and fares are based on your destination.

If you decide to take the train, always remember to keep your train ticket with you – it is required when leaving the station.

How can I get to...	...e wa donoyooni ikimasu ka?	...へは どのように 行きますか？
Tokyo	Tookyoo	東京
Osaka	Oosaka	大阪

What time does the bus leave?	Basu wa nanji ni shyuppatsu shimasu ka?	バスは何時に 出発しますか？
What time does the train leave?	Denshya wa nanji ni shyuppatsu shimasu ka?	電車は何時に 出発しますか？
How much is the ticket?	Kippu wa ikura desu ka?	きっぷはいくら ですか？
I want to rent a car.	Rentakaa o karitai desu.	レンタカーを 借りたいです。
I want to buy a train ticket.	Denshya no kippu o kaitai desu.	電車のきっぷを 買いたいです。
I want to take a taxi.	Takushii ni noritai desu.	タクシーに乗り たいです。
...ticket(s) please.	*...kippu o onegai shimasu.*	切符をお願い します。
One	Ichimai	1枚
Two	Nimai	2枚
Three	Sanmai	3枚
Four	Yonmai	4枚
One round-trip please.	Oofuku kippu o ichimai kudasai.	往復切符を一 枚下さい。

TAKING A TAXI

Narita International Airport is situated approximately 60 km from central Tokyo. Traffic is usually poor and therefore taking a taxi to the city could run you well over one hundred dollars with tolls. No wonder most people use the train or bus service.

CHAPTER FOUR

At the hotel

REGISTRATION

If you are staying somewhere other than a western-style hotel, here are some phrases that will help you. Try visiting a Japanese inn "ryokan" or stay at a hot spring "onsen" for a day or two if your schedule permits. There you'll experience traditional style accommodations, food and hospitality.

I have a reservation.	Yoyaku o shite imasu.	予約をしています。
I do not have a reservation.	Yoyaku wa shite imasen.	予約はしていません。
I would like to make a reservation.	Yoyaku o onegai shimasu.	予約をお願いします。
My name is... (last name)	Watashi no namae wa ...desu.	私の名前は...です。
I would like a room ...	*...beya o onegai shimasu.*	...部屋をお願いします。
with a double bed	Daburu beddo no	ダブルベッドの
with a twin	Tsuin no	ツインの
with a shower	Shyawaa tsuki no	シャワー付きの
facing the street	Toori ni menshita	通りに面した

22

facing the ocean	Umigawa no	海側の
facing the mountains	Yamagawa no	山側の
for tonight	Konya	今夜
for one night	Ippakku	1泊
for two nights	Nihaku	2泊
for one week	Isshyukan	1週間
for two weeks	Nishyukan	2週間
How much is it?	Ikura desu ka?	いくらですか？
What floor is it on?	Nankai desu ka?	何階ですか？
How do I get to my room?	Donoyooni heya ni ikimasu ka?	どのように部屋に行きますか？
Is there an elevator?	Erebeetaa wa arimasu ka?	エレベーターはありますか？
May I see the room?	Heya o misete moraemasu ka?	部屋を見せてもらえますか？
I would like a…	*…ni shitai desu.*	…にしたいです。
bigger room	Ookina heya	大きな部屋
cheaper room	Yasui heya	安い部屋
quieter room	Shizukana heya	静かな部屋
I need some help with my bags.	Nimotsu o hakobu no o tetsudatte kudasai.	荷物を運ぶのを手伝ってください。
Do you have a safety deposit box?	Kichoohin ire wa arimasu ka?	貴重品入れはありますか？

Please put this in your safety deposit box.	Kichoohin o azukatte kudasai.	貴重品を預かってください。
I would like to get something from my safety deposit box.	Kichoohin ire kara toridashitai mono ga arimasu.	貴重品入れから取り出したい物があります。

HOTEL SERVICES

All service charges will be included in your bill. Therefore a simple thank you is all that is necessary to show your appreciation after receiving someone's assistance.

Could you wake me at … please?	*Mooningu cooru o … ni onegai shimasu.*	モーニングコールを…にお願いします。
6 o'clock	rokuji	6時
7 o'clock	shichiji	7時
8 o'clock	hachiji	8時
I need…	*…ga hoshii desu.*	…がほしいです。
an extra bed	Moo hitotsu beddo	もう1つベッド
another blanket	Moo ichimai moofu	もう1枚毛布
another pillow	Moo hitotsu makura	もう1つ枕
some towels	Taoru	タオル
some toilet paper	Toiretto peepaa	トイレットペーパー
some soap	Sekken	せっけん
some shampoo	Shyanpuu	シャンプー
I need something dry-cleaned.	Kuriiningu o onegai shimasu.	クリーニングをお願いします。
I need this repaired.	Shyuuri o onegai shimasu.	修理をお願いします。

Where is the nearest ...?	*Ichiban chikai ...* *wa doko desu ka?*	一番ちかい...は どこですか？
pharmacy	yakkyoku	薬局
post office	yuubinkyoku	郵便局
public telephone	kooshyudenwa	公衆電話
shopping mall	shoppingu mooru	ショッピングモール
subway station	chikatetsu no eki	地下鉄の駅
Please send someone, I am having a problem with the...	*... no mondai ga arimasu node donataka heya ni kite kudasai.*	...の問題があります ので、どなたか部屋に 来て下さい。
air conditioner	Eakon	エアコン
television	Terebi	テレビ
heat	Danboo	暖房
lights	Denki	電気
window	Mado	窓
There's not enough hot water.	Oyu ga demasen.	お湯がでません。
How do I make a... call?	*... wa donoyoo ni kakemasu ka?*	...はどのようにかけ ますか？
local	Gaisen	外線
long-distance	Enkyori denwa	遠距離電話
collect	Korekuto kooru	コレクトコール
overseas	Kokusai denwa	国際電話

Purchase a telephone card for 500 or 1000 yen. They are very handy, attractive and make nice additions to your photo album. These cards can be used with most public telephones. After lifting the receiver place the card in the slot face up. Begin dialing once you here a dial tone. The card will eject automatically after you hang up. Remember to include the area code if you are dialing a number outside of the city you are in. Tokyo is 03, Osaka 06.

ANSWERING THE DOOR

Who is it?	Donata desu ka?	どなたですか？
Just a minute.	Chotto matte kudasai.	ちょっと待って 下さい。
Please come back later.	Atode mata kite kudasai.	後でまた来て下さい。
Come in.	Haitte kudasai.	入ってください。
Please leave it on the table.	Teeburu ni oite kudasai.	テーブルに置いて ください。
Thank you.	Arigatoo.	ありがとう。

CHECKING OUT

| What time is check-out? | Chekku auto wa nanji desu ka? | チェックアウトは 何時ですか？ |
| I would like to check out. | Chekku auto o onegai shimasu. | チェックアウトを お願いします。 |

I am leaving...	...shyuppatsu shimasu	...出発します。
tomorrow	Ashita(Asu)	明日
today	Kyoo	今日
on Sunday	Nichiyoobi ni	日曜日に
Please send someone for my bags.	Nimotsu o torini kite kudasai.	荷物を取りに来て下さい。
Thank you. I had a great time.	Totemo tanoshikatta desu. Arigatoo	とても楽しかったです。ありがとう。

SOLVING PROBLEMS

I think there is a mistake on my bill.	Kono keisansho wa machigatteiru to omoimasu.	この計算書は間違っていると思います。
I did not ...	Watashi wa...imasen.	私は...いません。
make any phone calls.	denwa o kakete	電話をかけて
watch a movie	eiga o mite	映画を見て
have any drinks from the in-room bar.	reizooko no nomimono o nonde	冷蔵庫の飲み物を飲んで
order room service.	ruumusaabisu o tanonde	ルームサービスをたのんで
eat at this restaurant.	kokono resutoran de tabete	ここのレストランで食べて
I would like to speak to the manager please.	Shihainin no kata to ohanashi sasete kudasai.	支配人の方とお話しさせてください。
I want to complain about the...	...ni tsuite kujo ga arimasu.	...について苦情があります。
noise	Sooon	騒音
service	Saabisu	サービス
food	Tabemono	食べ物

27

CHAPTER FIVE

Travelling in Japan

Most people travelling in Japan find public transportation to be more than adequate. Do not be intimidated by the complex appearance of the train system maps. Many visitors are overwhelmed by the number of different train lines; however, each line has a distinctive color that is illustrated on all train maps. In major cities you will find each station clearly marked in English. Pick up an English train map from any tourist information office or purchase one at any large bookstore in Japan.

TRAINS

Local train tickets are purchased at vending machines near the entrance of each train line. Maps are situated above the machines that specify the fares to each station. When in doubt, purchase the lowest fare and pay the difference at the end of your trip by using the fare adjustment machines before leaving the station.

Most stations are equipped with an automated ticket-taking machine. Place your ticket in the machine, continue walking through and pick up your ticket at the other end. Always remember to hold on to your ticket since you will need it when leaving the station.

Avoid using trains during rush hour. Trains are unbearably crowded as most people use the train to commute to work or school.

When travelling long distances use the bullet train (Shinkansen). Tourist can benefit from the use of a JR Rail Pass that you purchase from your travel agent in Canada. The pass allows unlimited usage of all Japan Rail trains for a period specified by you. Purchasing this pass is well worth the money if you plan on visiting areas of Japan outside Tokyo.

Excuse me, where is the closest ...?	*Sumimasen ichiban chikai ... wa doko desu ka?*	すみません、 いちばん近い ... は どこですか？
subway station	chikatetsu no eki	地下鉄の駅
Japan Rail station	JR no eki	JRの駅
Where can I buy a train ticket?	Kippu wa doko de kaemasu ka?	切符はどこで 買えますか？
I want to go to...	... e ikitai desu.	...へ行きたいです。
How much is it to...?	... made ikura desu ka?	...までいくらですか？
What time does the train leave at?	Denshya wa nanji ni shyuppatsu shimasu ka?	電車は何時に 出発しますか？
What track does the train leave from?	Densha wa nanban sen kara demasu ka?	電車は何番線から 出ますか？
Do I have to change lines?	Norikae ga hitsuyoo desu ka?	乗り換えが必要 ですか？
How long does it take?	Donokurai jikan ga kakarimasu ka?	どのくらい時間 がかかりますか？
Is it an express train?	Kono denshya wa kaisoku (kyuukoo) desu ka?	この電車は快速 （急行）ですか？
What time is the...?	*... wa nanji desu ka?*	...は何時ですか？
first train	Shihatsu denshya	始発電車
last train	Saishyu denshya	最終電車

29

next train	Tsugi no denshya	次の電車
Where is the exit?	Deguchi wa doko desu ka?	出口はどこ ですか？
Where is the Yamanote line?	Yamanotesen wa doko desu ka?	山手線はどこ ですか？
Does this train stop at...?	Kono denshya wa...ni tomarimasu ka?	この電車は...に とまりますか？
What is the next station?	Tsugi no eki wa nan desu ka?	次の駅は何ですか？
I want a(n)...	*...o onegai shimasu.*	...をおねがいします。
non-smoking seat	Kinen seki	禁煙席
non-reserved seat	Jiyuu seki	自由席
reserved seat	Shitee seki	指定席
smoking seat	Kitsuen seki	喫煙席
one-way ticket	Katamichi kippu	片道切符
round-trip ticket	Oofuku kippu	往復切符
aisle seat	Tsuurogawa no seki	通路側の席
window seat	Madogawa no seki	窓側の席

Using public washrooms

Western-style toilets can be found in department stores and hotels. Remember to carry a hand-kerchief with you because most washrooms do not have paper towels or hand dryers.

Problems

Excuse me, can you help me?	Sumimasen, tasukete moraemasu ka?	すみません、たすけてもらえますか？
Do you speak any English?	Eigo o hanasemasu ka?	英語を話せますか？
I lost my ticket.	Kippu o nakushimashita.	切符をなくしました。
I took the wrong train.	Chigau denshya ni notte shimaimashita.	違う電車に乗ってしまいました。
When is the next train?	Tsugi no denshya wa itsu demasu ka?	次の電車はいつ出ますか？

TRAIN STATION SIGNS

地下鉄	subway
JR駅	Japan Rail station
きっぷ売場	ticket vending
改札口	ticket gate
入口	entrance
出口	exit
中央口	central entrance/exit
北口	north entrance/exit
東口	east entrance/exit
南口	south entrance/exit
西口	west entrance/exit
1番線	track no. 1
トイレ	toilet (washrooms)

TAKING THE SUBWAY

After a few hours of riding the subway system, you should have little difficulty getting from one place to the next. All trains and stations are marked using a color system so that passengers can easily tell one line from another. To change train lines, use your train map to find the fastest route to your destination. In most cases you will not have to leave the station to transfer to another line. For stations that require passengers to exit and re-enter at another ticket gate, you must show your ticket to the attendant before entering. Avoid using the automated ticket machines when transferring between lines.

TAKING THE BUS

There are two systems for paying fares on city buses. In Tokyo, most city buses require passengers to pay at the front of the bus upon boarding. The fare is the same regardless of the distance you are travelling. Some bus lines however, require passengers to pay at the end of their ride. Passengers must take a ticket when entering the bus using the rear doors. The fare is calculated according to the distance travelled and is paid when getting off at the front of the bus. Most buses are equipped with machines that provide change.

Getting off at your stop on a crowded train can sometimes pose a problem. If you find yourself in this situation say "orimasu" which means, "I'm getting off the train!" Passengers will try to move to one side in order to let you pass.

Do you stop at...?	...ni tomarimasu ka?	...に止まりますか？
Please let me know when I reach my stop.	Watashi no oriru tokoro de oshiete kudasai.	私の降りる所で教えてください。
Excuse me, when is the next bus?	Sumimasen, tsugi no basu wa itsu desu ka?	すみません、次のバスはいつですか？
Excuse me, what bus do I take to go to ...	Sumimasen,...e wa dono basu de ikemasu ka?	すみません、...へはどのバスで行けますか？

TAXIS

In most situations you will find the trains to be your best bet for travel, however if you need to take a taxi, keep in mind that they are expensive. Taxis can be flagged down on the street or at taxi stands located near train stations and hotels. The taxi driver will open and close the door for you by using a lever from the inside. You need not tip the driver nor negotiate the fare. Passengers are required only to pay the amount that appears on the meter at the end of the ride. The only exception is when using the expressway; then you must pay for all tolls.

Please call a taxi.	Takushi o yonde kudasai.	タクシーを呼んでください。
I want to go...	*... ikitai desu.*	...行きたいです。
to the (Westin) hotel	(Uestyin) hoteru e	（ウエスティン）ホテルへ
to (Shinjuku)	(Shinjuku) e	（新宿）へ
Please...	*...kudasai*	...ください。
take the expressway	Koosokudooro o tsukatte	高速道路を使って
hurry	Isoide	急いで

33

go straight	Massugu ni itte	まっすぐに行って
turn left	Hidari ni magatte	左に曲がって
turn right	Migi ni magatte	右に曲がって
stop here	Kokode tomatte	ここでとまって
stop over there	Asoko de tomatte	あそこでとまって
wait here	Kokode matte ite	ここで待っていて
How much is it?	Ikura desu ka?	いくらですか？
Keep the change.	Otsuri wa kekkoo desu.	おつりは結構です。
May I have a receipt?	Ryooshyusho o moraemasu ka?	領収書をもらえますか？

DRIVING YOURSELF

You may want to think twice about getting behind the wheel in Japan. The roads are very narrow and usually congested in the city, not to mention the fact that everyone drives on the left side of the road, as in Britain. Fuel is expensive and parking is limited. But if you insist on renting a car, here are a few phrases that will get you on your way.

RENTING A CAR

I would like to rent a...	*...o karitai desu.*	...を借りたいです。
compact car	Kogatashya	小型車
mid-size car	Chuugatashya	中型車
full-size car	Ookime no kuruma	大きめの車
van	Wagonshya	ワゴン車
Is the car...?	*Sonokuruma wa... desu ka?*	その車は...ですか
automatic	ootomatikku	オートマティク
standard	manyuaru	マニュアル

What kind of car is it?	Kuruma no shyurui wa nan desu ka?	車の種類はなんですか？
What colors do you have?	Nani iro ga arimasu ka?	何色がありますか？
Does the car have ...?	*Kuruma ni ... wa tsuiteimasu ka?*	車に...はついていますか？
air bags	eaa baggu	エアーバッグ
a child seat	chyrudo shiito	チャイルドシート
cruise control	kuruuzu kontorooru	クルーズコントロール
power steering	pawaa sutearingu	パワーステアリング
power brakes	pawaa bureeki	パワーブレーキ
a cassette player	kasetto dekki	カセットデッキ
I need a car for...	*... kan kuruma o karitai desu.*	...間、車を借りたいです。
two days	Futsuka	2日
three days	Mikka	3日
one week	Isshyukan	1週間
I need a car for the weekend.	Shyumatsu ni kuruma o karitai desu.	週末に車を借りたいです。
I need a car for one day	Ichinichi kuruma o karitai desu.	1日車を借りたいです。

How much is it for...?	*...de ikura desu ka?*	...でいくらですか？
one day	Ichinichi	1日
two days	Futsukakan	2日間
three days	Mikkakan	3日間
one week	Isshyukan	1週間
the weekend	Shyumatsu	週末
How much mileage is included?	Nankiro made ryookin ni fukumarete imasu ka?	何キロまで料金に含まれていますか？
How much is it for each kilometre over?	Seigen kiro o koetara, ichikiro wa ikura desu ka?	制限キロを越えたら、1キロはいくらですか？
What are the different types of insurance?	Donna chigai no hoken ga arimasu ka?	どんな違いの保険がありますか？
When must I return the car?	Itsu made ni kaesanakute wa narimasen ka?	いつまでに返さなくてはなりませんか？
Do you have any English road maps?	Eigo no chizu wa arimasu ka?	英語の地図はありますか？
Should I return the car with a full tank of gas?	Gasorine wa mantan ni shite kaesu no desu ka?	ガソリンは満タンにして返すのですか？
Where do I return the car?	Kuruma wa doko de kaeshimasu ka?	車はどこで返しますか？

At the gas station

Fill it up please.	Mantan ni shite kudasai.	満タンにして下さい。
20 litres of regular gas please.	Regyuraa no gasorin o nijuu rittaa onegai shimasu.	レギュラーのガソリンを20リッターお願いします。
20 litres of premium gas please.	Haioku gasorin o nijuu rittaa onegai shimasu.	ハイオクガソリンを20リッターお願いします。
Please check the...	*...o tenken shite... kudasai.*	を点検してください。
oil	oiru	オイル
tires	taiya	タイヤ
How do I get to...?	...e wa donoyooni ikimasu ka?	...へはどのように行きますか？

CHAPTER SIX

Sightseeing

You will never run out of things to see and do in Japan. Plan your days carefully so that you do not miss out on all the wonderful sights. More often than not, trains will take you where you want to go. Fares can be quite expensive so if you think you will be travelling a lot, it is well worth the money to pick up a rail pass before leaving Canada.

If your time is limited in Japan, be sure to take a guided bus tour. Also, check to see if there are any festivals happening during your stay. They are well worth seeing!

Festivals – *matsuri* – can take the form of a celebration at a shrine, temple or within a town, city or village. One of the major features of many festivals is the *omikoshi*, a portable shrine that is carried on the shoulders of the participants. Festivals take place all year round most, commemorating historical and religious events.

Where is the tourist office?	Kankoo annaijo wa doko desu ka?	観光案内所は どこですか？
Could you please recommend some places to visit?	Kankoo o suru noni osusume no basho wa doko desu ka?	観光をするのに お勧めの場所 はどこですか？
Do you have English maps?	Eigo no chizu wa arimasu ka?	英語の地図は ありますか？
Where is…?	…wa doko desu ka?	…はどこですか？

How do you get to…?	…e wa donoyooni ikimasu ka?	…へはどのように いきますか？
How far is…from here?	…e wa kokokara donokurai kakarimasu ka?	…へはここから どのくらい かかりますか？
I'm lost.	Michi ni mayoi mashita.	道に迷いました。
How do I get back to…	…e wa donoyooni modorimasu ka?	…へはどのよう に戻りますか？
What is the fastest way to…	…e ichiban hayai ikikata wa nan desu ka?	…へ一番はやい行き 方はなんですか？
What is the closest station to…?	…e ichiban chikai eki wa doko desu ka?	…へ一番近い駅は どこですか？
What bus should I take to go to…?	…e wa dono basu ni notte ikimasu ka?	…へはどのバスに乗 って行きますか？
What time does the… leave?	*…wa nanji ni shyuppatsu shimasu ka?*	…は何時に出発 しますか？
bus	Basu	バス
train	Denshya	電車
I want to visit…	*…e ikitai desu.*	…へ行きたいです。
the Tokyo Dome	Tookyoo doomu	東京ドーム
Disneyland	Dizuniirando	ディズニーランド
Mt. Fuji	Fuji san	富士山
Osaka	Oosaka	大阪
a temple	Tera	寺
Tokyo Tower	Tookyoo Tawaa	東京タワー

What time does it...?	*Nanji ni ... ka?*	何時に...か？
close	shimarimasu	閉まります
open	akimasu	開きます
How much is the admission?	Nyuujo-ryoo wa ikura desu ka?	入場料はいくら ですか？
What can I see there?	Nani o miru koto ga dekimasu ka?	何を見る事が できますか？
What can I do there?	Nani o suru koto ga dekimasu ka?	何をすることが できますか？

 Remember to always carry a camera with you. You never know when you will come across a group of sumo wrestlers or a Buddhist temple dating back thousands of years. If you forget to bring one along, pick up a disposable camera at a local convenience store. They're inexpensive but still take reasonable photos.

Can I take pictures?	Shyashin o totte mo ii desu ka?	写真を撮っても いいですか？
Excuse me, could you please take a picture for me?	Sumimasen, shyashin o totte moraemasu ka?	すみません、写真を 撮ってもらえま すか？
What is the name of this...?	*Kono ... no namae wa nan desu ka?*	この...の名前は 何ですか？
building	tatemono	建物
dish	ryoori	料理
lake	mizuumi	湖

shrine	jinja	神社
station	eki	駅
store	mise	店
temple	tera	寺
town	machi	町
village	mura	村
What is that?	Are wa nan desu ka?	あれは何ですか？
When was it built?	Itsu tateraremashita ka?	いつ建てられました か？
What is it made from?	Nani de dekite imasu ka?	何でできています か？
What is it used for?	Nani ni tsukaimasu ka?	何に使いますか？
How did they make it?	Donoyooni tsukurimashita ka?	どのように 作りましたか？
What are they doing?	Nani o shite imasu ka?	何をしていますか？

Try attending a *kabuki* performance; traditional Japanese dance/theater. Performances are usually twice daily. To help you follow along, earphones with English explanations are available for foreign guests.

AREAS NOT TO BE MISSED

In and around Tokyo, be sure to visit the Imperial Palace, the home of Japan's emperor and imperial family. Visitors are not allowed inside, but are welcome to take pictures and visit the gardens surrounding the palace. Tokyo Disneyland, Asakusa and Meiji-jingu shrine are other areas you may want to consider visiting.

Those interested in sports should take in a baseball game and watch the popular Tokyo Giants play or see a traditional sumo tournament if one is happening during your visit.

In Tokyo, if you are looking to do some shopping visit areas such as; Ginza, Harajuku, Shinjuku, Shibuya, Ueno or Ikebukuro. Depending on what you are looking for you will find some areas more to your liking. Avoid shopping on weekends to miss the crowds.

OUTSIDE TOKYO

Take a trip to Kamakura and see the wonderful Buddhist temples and Shinto shrines, spend a day in Hakone or have Chinese food in Yokohama's Chinatown. All three areas are well worth the short trip.

If you have more than a day and you are looking for an interesting place to visit, try Karuizawa. Accessible by train, this area is a common vacation spot for the Japanese in the summer. Here you can enjoy many kinds of outdoor activities such as tennis, golf, cycling and horse riding.

Another extremely popular vacation area is the Izu peninsula, noted for its many hot springs. This resort area offers nice beaches and very attractive scenery.

CHAPTER SEVEN

Dining out and nightlife in Japan

There are many wonderful restaurants in Japan, but ordering can sometimes present some challenges. If you are having difficulty ordering, take advantage of the plastic food models that are usually displayed at the front of the restaurant by pointing to the item that you want. Remember, the gratuity is always included in the bill, so it is not necessary to leave a tip at any time.

GENERAL EXPRESSIONS

I'm hungry.	Onaka ga suite imasu.	おなかがすいて います。
I'm thirsty.	Nodo ga kawaite imasu.	のどがかわいて います。
Please recommend a good restaurant to have...	*...no oishii resutoran o oshiete kudasai.*	...のおいしいレストラ ンをおしえてくだ さい。
Japanese food	Washyoku	和食
Italian food	Itaria ryoori	イタリア料理
French food	Furansu ryoori	フランス料理
American-style food	Amerikan ryoori	アメリカン料理
breakfast	Chooshyoku	朝食
lunch	Ranchi	ランチ
dinner	Dinaa	ディナー

Is it expensive?	Takai desu ka?	高いですか？
Where is it located?	Sore wa doko ni arimasu ka?	それはどこに ありますか？
Do you need a reservation?	Yoyaku ga hitsuyoo desu ka?	予約が必要ですか？
I'd like to make a reservation for...	*...de Yoyaku o onegai shimasu.*	...で予約をおねがい します。
tonight	Konban	今晩
tommorow night	Ashita no yoru	明日の夜
two people	Futari	2人
six o'clock	Rokuji	6時
seven o'clock	Shichiji	7時
My name is ... I have a resevation.	Yoyaku o shite imasu ... desu.	予約をしています ...です。
I would like to sit...	*...no seki o onegai shimasu.*	...の席をお願い します。
in the non-smoking section	Kinen	禁煙
smoking section	Kitsuen	喫煙
at the counter	Kado	かど
by the window	Madogawa	窓側
in the tatami (rush grass mat) room	Washitsu(Zashiki) no heya	和室（座敷） の部屋

Noodles

Undoubtedly, ramen or Chinese noodle soup is one of Japan's most popular fast foods. It is often served with fried dumpling called *gyoza*. Ramen is great for lunch. Give it a try!

If you are the adventurous type, visit a sushi bar and try all the various types of raw fish. Here are a few popular ones you may want to try.

SUSHI

cucumber roll	kappa maki	かっぱ巻き
egg	tamago	たまご
eel	unagi	うなぎ
octopus	tako	たこ
red snapper	tai	たい
salmon	sake	さけ
shrimp	ebi	えび
squid	ika	いか
tuna	maguro	まぐろ
tuna belly	toro	とろ
yellow tail	hamachi	はまち
salmon roe	ikura	いくら
tuna roll	tekka maki	てっか巻き

ORDERING

At some fast food restaurants, customers purchase food tickets from a vending machine upon entering. The machine provides the appropriate change along with food tickets that must be presented at the counter or at your table.

At regular restaurants, you can get the attention of the server by simply raising your hand and saying "sumimasen," excuse me!

Excuse me!	Sumimasen!	すみません！

May I have (a)...	*...o kudasai*	を下さい。
ashtray	Haizara	灰皿
menu	Menyuu	メニュー
glass of water	Mizu	水
glass of white wine	Gurasu de shiro wain	グラスで白ワイン
glass of red wine	Gurasu de aka wain	グラスで赤ワイン
beer	Biiru	ビール
cup of coffee	Koohii	コーヒー
cup of tea	Koocha	紅茶
refill	Okawari	おかわり
I'd like to order please.	Chuumon o onegai shimasu.	注文をお願いします。
Excuse me, what do you recommend?	Sumimasen osusume wa nan desu ka?	すみません、お勧めはなんですか？
I need a...	*...ga hoshi desu.*	...がほしいです。
fork	Fooku	フォーク
knife	Naifu	ナイフ
spoon	Spoon	スプーン
napkin	Napukin	ナプキン
toothpick	Tsuma yooji	つまようじ
I don't eat...	*...wa taberaremasen*	...は食べられません。
raw fish	Osashimi	お刺し身
meat	Niku	肉
dairy	Nyuuseehin	乳製品
eggs	Tamago	卵

I would like …	*… o onegai shimasu.*	…をおねがいします。
the tempura combo	Tenpura teeshyoku	てんぷら定食
lunch	ranchi	ランチ
the special	Supeshyaru	スペシャル

When eating with others, say "itadakimasu" before you begin your meal. This expression is used in a variety of situations and literally means, "I will receive." After the meal say "gochisoosama desita" which means, "thank you, I enjoyed the meal."

Please bring more…	*Motto… o onegai shimasu.*	もっと…をおねがいします。
bread	pan	パン
beer	biiru	ビール
butter	bataa	バター
coffee	koohii	コーヒー
tea	koocha	紅茶
Do you have vegetarian dishes?	Yasai dake no ryoori wa arimasu ka?	野菜だけの料理はありますか？
Excuse me, what is this?	Sumimasen, kore wa nan desu ka?	すみません,これは何ですか？

Problems

I did not order this.	Kore wa tanonde imasen.	これは頼んでいません。
Please check on my order.	Mooichido watashi no chuumon o shirabete kudasai.	もう一度私の注文を調べて下さい。

This is too ...	*Kore wa totemo...desu.*	これはとても...です。
cold	tsumetai	冷たい
spicy	karai	辛い
salty	shyoppai	しょっぱい
This is too rare.	Kore wa mada nama desu.	これはまだ生 です。
This is overcooked.	Kore wa yakisugi desu.	これは焼きすぎです。
This... is not clean.	*Kono...wa kitanai desu.*	この...は汚いです。
cup	kappu	カップ
glass	koppu	コップ
dish	osara	お皿
fork	fooku	フォーク
spoon	spoon	スプーン
table	teeburu	テーブル
Where is the washroom?	Toire wa doko desu ka?	トイレはどこ ですか？
Could I have some...	*...o moraemasu ka?*	...をもらえますか？
bread	pan	パン
butter	bataa	バター
ketchup	kechappu	ケチャップ
pepper	koshyoo	こしょう
salt	shio	塩
soya sauce	shooyu	しょうゆ
sugar	satoo	砂糖

I'm full.	Onaka ga ippai desu.	お腹がいっぱいです。
Nothing else.	Moo nani mo irimasen.	もう何もいりませ
Thank you.	Arigatoo.	ん、ありがとう。
Cheque please.	Okanjoo o onegai shimasu.	お勘定をおねがい します。

In most restaurants, after receiving the bill, you pay as you leave. Most restaurants have a cashier set up near the exit. Do not leave money at your table.

Japanese cuisine

Here is a brief explanation of various traditional Japanese dishes.

Sukiyaki: Thinly sliced pieces of beef and cut vegetables cooked in an iron pan at your table. This dish is usually enjoyed with a raw egg as a dipping sauce.

Tempura: Fish, shrimp, and vegetables battered and deep fried in vegetable oil. Served with steamed rice and a dipping sauce.

Nabe: A large pot with cut vegetables, tofu, thinly sliced beef, chicken or seafood cooked together in a broth and brought to a boil. This popular dish is most popular during the winter time.

Yakitori: Chunks of chicken barbecued on bamboo skewers. Also beef, pork, liver and vegetables can be prepared in the same way. Yakitori restaurants are usually very lively and inexpensive.

FOOD DICTIONARY

BREAKFAST
Western breakfast

fried eggs	medama yaki	目玉焼き
scrambled eggs	sukuranburu eggu	スクランブルエッグ
boiled eggs	yude tamago	ゆで卵
bacon	beekon	ベーコン
sausage	sooseeji	ソーセージ
pancakes	hottokeeki	ホットケーキ
cereal	koonfureeku	コーンフレーク
toast	toosuto	トースト
fruit	kudamono	果物
yogurt	yooguruto	ヨーグルト

Japanese breakfast

soybean (miso) soup	misoshiru	みそ汁
seaweed	nori	のり
steamed rice	gohan	ご飯
fried fish	yakizakana	焼き魚
pickled vegetable	tsukemono	漬け物
fermented bean	nattoo	納豆

Western lunch

sandwiches	sandoicchi	サンドイッチ
hamburgers	hanbaagaa	ハンバーガー

french fries	furaido poteto	フライドポテト
hot dogs	hottodokku	ホットドック
pizza	piza	ピザ

Japanese lunch

lunch box	bentoo	べんとう
riceball	onigiri	おにぎり
Japanese noodle	udon	うどん
noodle soup	raamen	ラーメン
fried rice	chaahan	チャーハン
fried dumplings	gyooza	餃子
curry with rice	kareeraisu	カレーライス
tempura on rice	tendon	天丼
fried rice omelet	omuraisu	オムライス

Western dinner

steak	suteeki	ステーキ
ribs	ribu	リブ
roast beef	roosuto biifu	ローストビーフ
chicken	chikin	チキン
spaghetti	supagettii	スパゲッティー
baked potato	beeku poteto	ベークポテト

Japanese dinner

A typical Japanese meal usually consists of a few dishes served with rice. Here are a few common ones.

bean cake (tofu)	toofu	とうふ
deep fried (chicken)	karaage	から揚げ
croquette	korokke	コロッケ
boiled seasoned vegetable	nimono	煮物
cooked meat and potato	nikujaga	肉じゃが
deep fried pork	tonkatsu	とんかつ
eel on rice	unagi donburi	うなぎ丼
pancake with pork and vegetable	okonomiyaki	お好み焼き
Japanese fried noodle	yakisoba	やきそば
sliced raw fish	sashimi	刺し身
chicken barbecued on a bamboo skewer	yakitori	やきとり
breaded shrimp	ebifurai	エビフライ
pickled vegetables	oshinko	お新香
stir-fried vegetable	yasaiitame	野菜炒め

NIGHTLIFE IN JAPAN

There are many districts of Tokyo that come to life at night. Roppongi for one is an area where many clubs, called discos in Japan, and bars are located. Most discos charge 3000 to 5000 yen to enter, which include tickets that can be redeemed for food and beverages. Many discos have a dress code, so do not wear jeans or running shoes if you plan to do some dancing. Bars in this area usually attract a younger crowd.

Another area of Tokyo you may want to visit at night is Ginza.

Many restaurants and bars can be found here. This district is more for the older traveler since the restaurants are more expensive.

Karaoke bars are also popular night spots. If you are uncomfortable about singing in public, visit a private karaoke box with friends. Here you can eat, drink and sing all your favorite songs of the past and present without feeling uneasy.

Keep in mind that all trains stop at around 12:30 to 1:00 a.m. If you plan to stay out late please be aware that taxi rates go up in the evening and you may find yourself waiting in line at a taxi stand.

I would like to go to a...	*...e ikitai desu.*	...へ行きたいです。
bar	Baa	バー
jazz bar	Jazu baa	ジャズバー
piano bar	Piano baa	ピアノバー
karaoke bar	Karaoke baa	カラオケバー
club	Disuko	ディスコ
What type of music do they play?	Donna kyoku ga kakarimasu ka?	どんな曲がかかりますか？
How can I get there?	Sokoe wa donoyooni ikimasu ka?	そこへは どのように行きますか？

Ordering a drink

May I have a... please?	*...o kudasai.*	...をください。
beer	Biiru	ビール
cocktail	Kakuteru	カクテル
a glass of white wine	Gurasu de shiro wain	グラスで白ワイン
a glass of red wine	Gurasu de aka wain	グラスで赤ワイン
glass of whiskey (on the rocks)	Uisukii (rokku de)	ウイスキー （ロックで）
glass of bourbon	Baabon	バーボン

Beware!

A night out on the town can leave you broke if you are not careful. Always ask how much things cost so that you don't find yourself spending more than you want to. Many clubs and bars have a sitting fee that is added to the bill. Places that do not openly display their prices should be avoided. As in most large cities there are certain districts that you should avoid. Find out where these areas are before you venture out.

CHAPTER EIGHT

Shopping

There are an unlimited number of places to shop in and around any major city. Large shopping districts are usually located near major train stations. Most anything can be found in these areas. Although some large stores offer duty free shopping, the best deals are to be made at markets and local malls. Prices are pretty firm, so don't haggle too much. A five percent consumption tax will be added at the cash register on most items.

Where is there a(n)...?	*...wa doko desu ka?*	...はどこですか？
bakery	Pan-ya	パン屋
bank	Ginkoo	銀行
bookstore	Hon-ya	本屋
department store	Depaato	デパート
drugstore	Yakkyoku	薬局
dry cleaner	Kuriiningu-ya	クリーニング屋
electronics store	Denki-ya	電気屋
grocery store	Suupaa maaketto	スーパーマーケット
liquor store	Saka-ya	酒屋
mall	Shyotengai	商店街
convenience store	kombiniensu sutoaa	コンビニエンス ストアー
souvenir store	Omiyage-ya	おみやげ屋

sporting goods store	Supootsu yoohin ten	スポーツ用品店
toy store	Omocha-ya	おもちゃ屋
Can you help me?	Tasukete kuremasu ka? (or) Sumimasen	たすけてくれ ますか？
I am looking for...	*...o sagashite imasu.*	...をさがしています。
a hat	booshi	帽子
a jacket	jaketto or (Uwagi)	ジャケット（上着）
a pair of pants	zubon	ズボン
a scarf	sukaafu	スカーフ
a shirt	shyatsu	シャツ
a skirt	sukaato	スカート
a pair of shoes	kutsu	くつ
a pair of socks	kutsushita	くつ下
some souvenirs	omiyage	お土産
a sweater	seetaa	セーター
a tie	nekutai	ネクタイ
a T-shirt	T-shyatsu	Ｔシャツ
an umbrella	kasa	傘
Do you have any others?	Hoka ni arimasu ka?	他にありますか？
Do you have something less expensive?	Nanika motto yasui mono wa arimasu ka?	何かもっと安いもの はありますか？
Do you have anything else that is similar to this?	Kore to nita mono de hoka ni arimasu ka?	これと似たもので 他にありますか？

What... does it come in?	Donna...ga arimasu ka?	どんな...があり ますか？
color	iro	色
size	saizu	サイズ
May I try it on?	Shichaku shitemo ii desu ka?	試着してもいい ですか？
Where are the changing rooms?	Shichaku shitsu wa doko desu ka?	試着室はどこ ですか？
Do you have a mirror?	Kagami wa arimasu ka?	鏡はありますか？
Is this on sale?	Kore wa baagen hin desu ka?	これはバーゲン品で すか？
How much does it cost?	Ikura shimasu ka?	いくらしますか？

When shopping for clothing always try things on before buying. Most stores do not allow exchanges or refunds.

Colors and sizes

Do you have it in ...?	Korede...wa arimasu ka?	これで...は ありますか？
beige	beeju	ベージュ
black	kuro	黒
blue	ao	青
brown	chairo	茶色
gray	guree	グレー

green	midori	緑
pink	pinku	ピンク
purple	murasaki	紫
red	aka	赤
white	shiro	白
yellow	kiiro	黄色
small	esu	S
medium	emu	M
large	eru	L
extra large	eru eru	L L

SIZE CHART

Women's clothing					
Japan	7	9	11	13	15
North America	8	10	12	14	16

Women's shoes					
Japan	22	23	24	25	26
North America	5	6	7	8	9

Men's shirts					
Japan	36	37	38	39	40
North America	14	14½	15	15½	16

Men's shoes					
Japan	24	25	26	27	28
North America	6	7	8	9	10

In Japan, many clothing companies manufacture a "free" size or what we refer to as one size fits all. Tags are marked with an F.

Material

I am looking for something in…	…no mono o sagashite imasu.	…の物をさがして います。
corduroy	koodyuroi	コーデュロイ
cotton	men	綿
denim	denimu	デニム
leather	kawa	皮
satin	saten	サテン
silk	shiruku	シルク
suede	sueedo	スエード
wool	ke	毛

Fitting problems

It doesn't fit.	Saizu ga aimasen.	サイズが合いません。
It fits well.	Saizu wa aimasu.	サイズは合います。
It's too …	…sugimasu.	…すぎます。
small	chiisa	小さ
big	ooki	大き
tight	kitsu	きつ
long	naga	長
short	mijika	短か

narrow	hoso	細
wide	hirogari	広がり

Do you have a...?	*...wa arimasu ka?*	...はありますか？
smaller size	chiisai saizu	小さいサイズ
larger size	ookii saizu	大きいサイズ

I'll take it.	Kore o kaimasu.	これを買います。

Do you take ...?	*...wa tsukaemasu ka?*	...は使えますか？
credit cards	kurejitto kaado	クレジットカード
traveller's cheques	toraberaazu chekku	トラベラーズチェック

ELECTRONICS STORES

If you are in the market for an electronic gadget, do shop around – prices vary greatly from store to store. Please keep in mind that the voltage is different in Canada and therefore most goods require the use of a transformer. Although slightly more expensive, some larger stores sell export models that have been made for Canada and the United States. Here you can try bargaining with the salesperson to get the best price possible.

I want to buy a...	*...o kaitai desu.*	...を買いたいです。
camera	kamera	カメラ
CD player	CD pureeyaa	CD プレイヤー
computer	konpyuutaa	コンピューター
electric razor	denki kamisori	電気かみそり
radio	rajio	ラジオ
stereo	sutereo	ステレオ
video camera	bideo kamera	ビデオカメラ
Walkman	Wookuman	ウォークマン

Can I use this in Canada?	Kore wa Kanada de tsukaemasu ka?	これはカナダで 使えますか？
What is the voltage?	Denatsu wa nan desu ka?	電圧は何ですか？
Do I need an adapter?	Adaputaa ga hitsuyoo desu ka?	アダプターが必要 ですか？
How long is the warranty?	Hoshoo kikan wa donokurai desu ka?	保証期間は どのくらいですか？
Can I take this to a dealer in Canada if I have a problem with it?	Moshi mondai ga okitara, Kanada ni aru omise ni motte ikemasu ka?	もし問題が起きたら カナダにある 店に持ってい けますか？
Please explain the functions.	Kinoo ni tsuite setsumei shite kudasai.	機能について説明 してください。
What is the difference between these two models?	Kono futatsu no moderu no chigai wa nan desu ka?	この二つのモデルの 違いはなん ですか？

 If you want to buy some inexpensive souvenirs for your friends and family back home, visit a 100 yen shop. Similar to dollar shops these stores sell a variety of Japanese items that make great gifts.

How many batteries does it take?	Denchi wa ikutsu hitsuyoo desu ka?	電池はいくつ必要 ですか？
What type of batteries does it take?	Dono denchi o tsukaimasu ka?	どの電池を使 いますか？
Where is this made?	Doko de tsukurareta seehin desu ka?	どこで作られた 製品ですか？

CHAPTER NINE

Phones, mail and money

TELEPHONE

Using public phones

There are many different types of public phones used in Japan. Be aware that not all public pay phones can be used to make overseas calls. Overseas telephones are clearly marked and calls can be made using your credit card. Prepaid telephone cards for 500, 1000 or 5000 yen or 10 and 100 yen coins can be used when making local calls. Make sure that you have enough units on your phone card (or coins handy) so that you do not get cut off.

Is there a public phone nearby?	Kooshyudenwa wa chikaku ni arimasu ka?	公衆電話は近くに ありますか？
May I use the phone?	Denwa o tsukattemo ii desu ka?	電話を使っても いいですか？
I'd like to make a... call.	*...denwa o kaketai desu.*	...電話をかけたい です。
local	Rookaru	ローカル
long distance	Enkyori	遠距離
overseas	Kokusai	国際
collect	Korekuto	コレクト
person-to-person	Aitesaki shitei	相手先指定

GENERAL EXPRESSIONS

Hello	Moshi-moshi	もしもし
May I speak with... please?	...san o onegai. shimasu	...さんをお願い します。
When will (he/she) return?	Itsu modorimasu ka?	いつ戻りますか？
Please ask (him/her) to call me back.	Denwa o hoshii to tsutaete kudasai.	電話をほしいと 伝えて下さい。
He (She) has my number.	Kare (kanojo) wa denwa bangoo o shitte imasu	彼（彼女）は電話 番号を知ってい ます。
My number is...(see numbers in Chapter 2)	Watashi no denwa bangoo wa... desu	私の電話番号は... です
Please tell (him/her) that I called.	Denwa ga atta koto o tsutaete kudasai.	電話があった事を 伝えて下さい。
I will call again, thank you.	Mata kakenaoshimasu, arigatoo.	またかけなおしま す、ありがとう。
Please speak...	*...de hanashite kudasai.*	...で話して下さい。
louder	ookinakoe	大きな声
slower	yukkuri	ゆっくり

AT THE POST OFFICE

Where is the nearest post office?	Ichiban chikai yuubin-kyoku wa doko desu ka?	一番近い郵便局 はどこですか？

I want to send...	*... okuritai desu.*	... 送りたいです。
this to Canada	kore o Kanada e	これをカナダへ
this envelope	kono fuusho o	この封書を
this letter	kono tegami o	この手紙を
this postcard	kono hagaki o	このハガキを
this package	kono nimotsu o	この荷物を
this by air mail	kore o kookuubin de	これを航空便で
this by surface mail	kore o funabin de	これを船便で
this by express mail	kore o sokutatsu de	これを速達で
I want to insure this.	Kore ni hoken o kaketai desu.	これに保険を かけたいです。
It is fragile.	Kowaremono desu.	こわれものです。
I want to buy some stamps.	Kitte o kudasai.	切手を下さい。

BANKING

Most banks are open from 9 to 3, Monday to Friday and closed on the weekends. Bank machines are open until 7 o'clock on weekdays and 2 o'clock on Saturdays in most cities.

Japanese currency

There are six coins used in Japanese currency; one, five, ten, fifty, one-hundred and five-hundred yen. Bills consist of one-thousand, five-thousand, and ten-thousand yen. Unlike a one-hundred dollar bill in Canada you will rarely have a problem getting change for a ten-thousand-yen bank note as they are commonly used in Japan.

Do you take foreign currency?	Gaikoku kawase o atsukatte imasu ka?	外国為替を扱っていますか？
I want to change… to yen.	*…o yen ni ryoogae shite kudasai.*	…を円に両替してください。
Canadian dollars	Kanada doru	カナダドル
American dollars	Amerika doru	アメリカドル
I want to change my traveller's cheques.	Toraberaazu chekku o ryoogae shite kudasai.	トラベラーズチェックを両替してください。
Is there a service charge?	Tesuuryoo wa kakarimasu ka?	手数料はかかりますか？
What is the exchange rate today?	Kyoo no reeto wa ikura desu ka?	今日のレートはいくらですか？

Cash and traveller's cheques can be changed at any authorized foreign exchange bank and at large hotels and stores. U.S. currency is widely accepted and can often be changed to Japanese yen at local banks.

CHAPTER TEN

Useful phrases for Canadian merchants

This chapter was written to help people who provide service to Japanese people visiting in Canada. In Japan, salespeople always greet their customers by saying "Irasshyaimase" (welcome). Try it! You'll always get a smile in return. Just be sure that the customer does, in fact, speak Japanese.

HELPING YOUR CUSTOMER

Welcome.	Irasshyaimase.	いらっしゃいませ。
Please look around.	Doozo gojiyuu ni mite kudasai.	どうぞ御自由に見てください。
Take your time.	Goyukkuri.	ごゆっくり。
Can I help you?	Nanika goyoo desu ka?	何かご用ですか？
Are you looking for something in particular?	Nanika tokubetsu ni osagashi desu ka?	何か特別におさがしですか？
Can I help you find a size?	Saizu o sagashimashyoo ka?	サイズをさがしましょうか？
What size are you looking for?	Dono saizu o osagashi desu ka?	どのサイズをおさがしですか？

Your Japanese customer may answer this question by saying, esu (S) which means small, emu (M), medium or eru (L), large.

This is on sale.	Kochira wa seeruhin desu.	こちらはセール品です。
It is regular price.	Kochira wa tsuujoo no nedan desu.	こちらは通常の値段です。
Is this for you?	Kochira wa gojibun de otsukai desu ka?	こちらはご自分でお使いですか？
Is this a gift?	Kochira wa purezento desu ka?	こちらはプレゼントですか？
What color are you looking for?	Nani iro o sagashite imasu ka?	何色をさがしていますか？
Would you like to try it on?	Shichaku shite mimasu ka?	試着してみますか？
The changing room is over there.	Shichakushitsu wa achira desu.	試着室はあちらです。
How did it fit?	Saizu wa aimashita ka?	サイズは合いましたか？
Would you like another size?	Hoka no saizu ni shimasu ka?	他のサイズにしますか？
I'm sorry, we don't have it in…	*Sumimasen,…wa arimasen.*	すみません、…はありません。
extra small	esu esu	SS
small	esu	S

medium	emu	**M**
large	eru	**L**

I'm sorry, we are sold out.	Sumimasen ga urikire desu.	すみませんが 売り切れです。
Would you like a…?	*…o irimasu ka?*	…をいりますか？
bag	fukuro	袋
box	hako	箱
How would you like to pay for this?	Donoyooni shiharaimasu ka?	どのように 支払いますか？
I'm sorry we don't take Master Card/Visa.	Sumimasen ga Masutaa Kaado/Biza wa tsukaemasen.	すみませんが マスターカード/ ビザは使えません。
Thank you. Please come again.	Arigatoo gozaimashita mata omachishite imasu.	ありがと うございました。 またお待ちして います。

RESTAURANT SERVICE

The following phrases will help you to serve your Japanese guests better.

Do you have a reservation?	Yoyaku ga arimasu ka?	予約がありますか？
How many people?	Nanmei desu ka?	何名ですか？
Smoking or non-smoking?	Kinen seki ni shimasu ka soretomo kitsuen seki ni shimasu ka?	禁煙席にしますか, それとも 喫煙席に しますか？

This way please.	Kochira desu.	こちらです。
Here is the menu.	Kochira ga menyuu desu.	こちらがメニューです。
Are you ready to order?	Chuumon o torimashyo ka?	注文を取りましょうか？
Can I get you something to drink?	Nanika nomimono o omochi shimasu ka?	何か飲み物をお持ちしますか？
Would you like an appetizer?	Zensai wa ikaga desu ka?	前菜はいかがですか？
Today's special is…	Honjitsu no supesharu wa…desu.	本日のスペシャルは…です。
How would you like your meat?	*Oniku no yakikagen wa doo shimasu ka?*	お肉の焼き加減はどうしますか？
rare	rea	レア
medium rare	midiamu rea	ミディアムレア
well done	ueru dan	ウエルダン
What kind of…would you like?	*Donna…ni shimasu ka?*	どんな…にしますか？
salad	sarada	サラダ
soup	suupu	スープ
dressing	doresshingu	ドレッシング
beer	biiru	ビール
wine	wain	ワイン
topping	toppingu	トッピング

Please help yourself.	Doozo gojiyuuni	どうぞ御自由に。
Here you are.	Hai doozo	はい、どうぞ。
How is everything?	Ikaga desu ka?	いかがですか？
Can I get you anything else?	Hoka ni nanika omochi shimasu ka?	他に何かお持ちしますか？
Would you like more...?	*Motto... o ikaga desu ka?*	もっと...をいかがですか？
beer	biiru	ビール
coffee	koohii	コーヒー
tea	koocha	紅茶
wine	wain	ワイン
juice	juusu	ジュース
bread	pan	パン
Would you like some dessert?	Dezaato wa ikaga desu ka?	デザートはいかがですか？
Would you like to take this home?	Omochi kaeri ni shimasu ka?	お持ち帰りにしますか？
Thank you.	Arigatoo gozaimashita.	ありがとうございました。

FOOD

fish	sakana	魚
shrimp	ebi	えび
crab	kani	かに
lobster	robusutaa	ロブスター

steak	suteeki	ステーキ
beef	gyuu-niku	牛肉
chicken	tori-niku	鳥肉
pork	buta-niku	豚肉
ribs	ribu	リブ
ham	hamu	ハム
roast beef	roosuto biifu	ローストビーフ
hamburger	hanbaagaa	ハンバーガー
mashed potatoes	mashyu poteto	マッシュポテト
baked potatoes	beeku poteto	ベークポテト
french fries	furaido poteto	フライドポテト
rice	raisu	ライス
bread	pan	パン
salad	sarada	サラダ
salad bar	sarada baa	サラダバー
vegetables	yasai	野菜
fruits	kudamono	くだもの
corn	toomorokoshi (koon)	とうもろこし（コーン）
carrots	ninjin	にんじん
egg	tamago	卵

BEVERAGES

Coke	koora	コーラ
milk	gyuunyuu	牛乳
juice	juusu	ジュース
water	mizu	水

beer	biiru	ビール
draft beer	nama biiru	生ビール
white wine	shiro wain	白ワイン
red wine	aka wain	赤ワイン
whiskey	uisukii	ウィスキー
cocktail	kakuteru	カクテル

Visiting Japan on business

In Japan, an exchange of business cards is the first step in the development of any business relationship. Therefore have plenty of business card with you during your visit – without one you will find it very difficult to make any headway. When giving your card, use both hands to hold the card at its corners while introducing yourself. When receiving someone's card, take it with both hands and place it on the table beside you. Never write on the card.

Remember to always address a Japanese person using his or her last name followed by *san*.

Greet all your Japanese counterparts by saying the following;

Nice to meet you, my name is Bill Smith	Hajimemashite, Bill Smith desu. Yoroshiku onegai shimasu.	はじめまして、 ビル・スミスです。 よろしくお願い します？
Here is my business card.	Korega watashi no meishi desu.	これが私の名刺 です。
Thank you for seeing me.	Oai dekite yokatta desu.	お会いできて よかったです。
I am here to see Mr. Tanaka.	Tanaka-san ni aini kimashita.	田中さんに会いに 来ました。

I have an appointment.	Yakusoku o shimashita.	約束をしました。
My appointment is at ... o'clock.	*...ji no yakusoku desu.*	...時の約束です。

9	Ku	9
10	Juu	10
11	Juu-ichi	11
1	Ichi	1
2	Ni	2
3	San	3
4	Yo	4

MAKING AN APPOINTMENT ON THE TELEPHONE

This is Bill Smith from XYZ Company. May I speak to Mr. Tanaka please?	XYZ no Bill Smith to iimasu ga, Tanaka-san o onegai shimasu.	XYZのビル・スミス と言いますが、田 中さんをお願いし ます？
When will he (she) return?	Kare (Kanajo) wa itsu modorimasu ka?	彼（彼女）はいつ 戻りますか？
I'll call again later.	Mata denwa shimasu.	また電話します。
Could you please tell him (her) that I called.	Denwa ga atta koto o kare (kanajo) ni tsutaete kudasai.	電話があった事を 彼（彼女）に伝え てください。
Could you please ask him (her) to call me.	Denwa ga hoshii to kare (kanajo) ni tsutaete kudasai.	電話がほしいと彼 （彼女）に伝えてくだ さい。
My phone number is ... (see numbers Chapter 2)	Watashi no denwa bangoo wa...desu.	私の電話 番号は...です。

I would like to make an appointment to meet with you.	Oaisuru apointo o torasete kudasai.	お会いするアポイントを取らせてください。
When are you available?	Itsu nara tsugoo ga ii desu ka?	いつなら都合がいいですか？
How about... at 1pm.	*...no ichiji wa doo desu ka?*	...の1時はどうですか？
Monday	Getsuyoo-bi	月曜日
Tuesday	Kayoo-bi	火曜日
Wednesday	Suiyoo-bi	水曜日
Thursday	Mokuyoo-bi	木曜日
Friday	Kinyoo-bi	金曜日
Where is your office located?	Kaishya no basho wa doko desu ka?	会社の場所はどこですか？
See you then.	Sore dewa, mata	それでは、また
Could we reschedule our appointment?	Yakusoku o kaete moraemasu ka?	約束を変えてもらえますか？
I'm having trouble finding your office.	Ofisu o mitsukeru koto ga dekimasen.	オフィスを見つけることができません。
What floor are you on?	Nankai desu ka?	何階ですか？

COMMON BUSINESS WORDS

appointment	apointo	アポイント
business card	meishi	名刺
business letter	bijinesu retaa	ビジネスレター

computer	konpyutaa	コンピューター
contract	keiyaku	契約
document	shorui	書類
estimate	mitsumori	見積もり
facsimile	fakkusu	ファックス
invest	tooshi	投資
invoice	seikyuushyo	請求書
meeting	kaigi	会議
negotiate	kooshoo	交渉
product	seihin	製品
project	keikaku	計画
service	saabisu	サービス
colleague	dooryoo	同僚
boss	jooshi	上司
secretary	hishyo	秘書

Language and cultural differences often pose problems for those trying to do business in Japan. Here are a few tips that might help you to be successful.

Although your Japanese counterpart may speak English well, it is important to have a translator present at important meetings. Also, all business presentation material should be translated into Japanese and presented in a professional manner. Keep in mind that most business decisions are often not made by one person but by a group of people. Decisions are often not made overnight, so please be patient when working with your Japanese associates.

CHAPTER TWELVE

Medical and emergency phrases

When travelling, remember to eat properly and get enough rest. It is easy to get caught up in all the excitement and neglect your health.

While the Japanese are traditionally very polite and honest people, travellers should always keep their belongings close by. Public areas such as shopping malls and trains are very crowded and pickpockets tend to linger in these areas. If an emergency arises, call 110 for the police or 119 for an ambulance. Public telephone have a one touch button so that you can easily report an emergency. You can also notify the police by going to a "police box" located near most train stations. A police box can be easily identified by the flashing red light.

Help!	Tasukete!	たすけて！
I don't feel well.	Kibun ga yokunai desu.	気分がよくないです。
I feel sick.	Kibun ga warui desu.	気分が悪い。
I feel dizzy.	Memai ga shimasu.	めまいがします。
I feel weak.	Karada ga yowatte imasu.	体が弱っています。
I feel tired.	Tsukareta kanji desu.	疲れた感じです。

I have …	*… desu.*	… です。
a broken bone	Kossetsu	骨折
a bruise	Daboku	打撲
a cold	Kaze	風邪
constipation	Benpi	便秘
diarrhea	Geri	下痢
a fever	Hatsunetsu	発熱
food poisoning	Shyokuchuudoku	食中毒
hay fever	Kafunshyo	花粉症
a headache	Atama ga itai	頭が痛い
indigestion	Shyokafuryoo	消化不良
insomnia	Fuminshyo	不眠症
a sore throat	Nodo ga itai	のどが痛い
a sprain	Nenza	ねんざ
a stomach ache	Onaka ga itai	おなかが痛い
a toothache	Ha ga itai	歯が痛い

I have a burn.	Yakedo o shimashita.	やけどをしました。
I have heartburn.	Muneyake ga shimasu.	胸やけがします。
I have a pain.	Itami ga arimasu.	痛みがあります。
I have a rash.	Hasshin ga deteimasu.	発疹が出ています。

My … hurts.	*Watashi no … ga itai desu.*	私の…が痛いです。
ankle	ashikubi	足首
arm	ude	腕
back	senaka	背中

chest	mune	胸
elbow	hiji	ひじ
finger	yubi	指
hand	te	手
leg	ashi	足
neck	kubi	首
shoulder	kata	肩
wrist	tekubi	手首

I lost my…	*…o nakushimashita.*	…をなくしました。
glasses	Megane	めがね
contact lenses	Kontakuto renzu	コンタクトレンズ
filling	Tsumeta ha	つめた歯

I need to see a…	*Watashi wa…ni mitemorai tai desu.*	私は…に診てもらいたいです。
doctor	isha	医者
dentist	haisha	歯医者
optometrist	meisha	眼医者

Please call a doctor!	Isha o yonde kudasai!	医者を呼んでください。
Where is the closest hospital?	Ichiban chikai byooin wa doko desu ka?	一番近い病院はどこですか？
Send an ambulance!	Kyuukyuushya o yonde kudasai!	救急車を呼んで下さい！
I need a doctor who speaks English.	Eigo no hanaseru isha ga hitsuyoo desu.	英語の話せる医者が必要です。

CONDITIONS

angina	Kyooshinshyo	狭心症
arthritis	Kansetsuen	関節炎
asthma	Zensoku	喘息
high blood pressure	Kooketsuatsu	高血圧
low blood pressure	Teiketsuatsu	低血圧
pregnant	Ninshin	妊娠
I am allergic to...	*Watashi wa...ni arerugii ga arimasu.*	私は...にアレルギーがあります。
antibiotics	kooseebushitsu	抗生物質
penicillin	penishirin	ペニシリン
I don't have any allergies.	Arerugii wa arimasen.	アレルギーはありません。
I take medication.	Kusuri o nondeimasu.	くすりをのんでイます。

Questions you may be asked by a doctor.

Where does it hurt?	Doko ga itamimasu ka?	どこが痛みますか？
When did it happen?	Itsu kara desu ka?	いつからですか？
How did it happen?	Donoyoo ni narimashita ka?	どのようになりましたか？
Do you have any allergies?	Arerugii wa arimasu ka?	アレルギーはありますか？
Are you taking any medication?	Ima nanika kusuri o nonde imasu ka?	今,何か薬をのんでいますか？

AT THE PHARMACY

Where is the pharmacy?	Yakkyoku wa doko desu ka?	薬局はどこですか？
I don't have a prescription.	Shyohoosen ga arimasen.	処方箋が ありません。
I need some medicine.	Kusuri o kudasai.	くすりをください。
What is the dosage?	Yooryoo wa nan desu ka?	用量はなんですか？

Things you may need

Make sure that you take a good supply of the medicines you need because the pharmacies in Japan will not have some products commonly found in Canada. This list should help you if the need for such items should arise.

aspirin	asupirin	アスピリン
bandages	bansookoo	ばんそうこう
cold medicine	kazegusuri	かぜ薬
contact lens cleaner	kontakuto renzu no kuriinaa	コンタクトレンズ のクリーナー
contact lens solution	kontakuto renzu hozoneki	コンタクトレンズ 保存液
cotton balls	kotton	コットン
diapers	omutsu	おむつ
hairspray	heaasupuree	ヘアースプレー
hand cream	hando kuriimu	ハンドクリーム
mouthwash	mausuwoshyu	マウスウォッシュ
powder	paudaa	パウダー
razor	kamisori	かみそり
hair conditioner	rinsu	リンス
sanitary napkins	seiri yoohin	生理用品

shampoo	shyanpuu	シャンプー
soap	sekken	石鹸
toothbrush	haburashi	歯ブラシ
toothpaste	hamigakiko	はみがき粉

EMERGENCIES REQUIRING THE POLICE

Call the police!	Keisatsu ni denwa shite kudasai!	警察に電話してください。
There has been an accident.	Jiko ga okimashita.	事故が起きました。
Fire!	Kaji!	火事！
Thief!	Doroboo!	どろぼう！
Where is the police station?	Kooban wa doko desu ka?	交番はどこですか？
I lost …	… o nakushi mashita.	…をなくしました。
Someone stole my…	*Darekaga watashi no … o nusumimashita.*	だれかが私の…を盗みました。
wallet	saifu	サイフ
camera	kamera	カメラ
credit cards	kurejitto kaado	クレジットカード
bag	bakku	バック
money	okane	お金
purse	kaban	かばん
passport	pasupooto	パスポート
traveller's cheques	toraberaazu chekku	トラベラーズチェック

If you lose your passport or for emergencies that require the
Canadian authorities contact:

Canadian Embassy

7-3-38 Akasaka, Minato-ku, Tokyo

Tel: 03(3408)2101

Canadian Consulate

2-2-3 Nishi shinsaibashi, Chuo-ku, Osaka

Tel: 06(6212)4910

OVER 100 CLASSIC COLES NOTES ARE ALSO AVAILABLE:

SHAKESPEARE

- Antony and Cleopatra
- Antony and Cleopatra
  Questions & Answers
- As You Like it
- Hamlet
- Hamlet in Everyday English
- Hamlet – Questions & Answers
- Julius Caesar
- Julius Caesar in Everyday English
- Julius Caesar
  Questions & Answers
- King Henry IV – Part 1
- King Henry V
- King Lear
- King Lear in Everyday English
- King Lear – Questions & Answers
- Macbeth
- Macbeth in Everyday English
- Macbeth – Questions & Answers
- Measure for Measure
- Merchant of Venice
- Merchant of Venice
  in Everyday English
- Midsummer Night's Dream
- Midsummer Night's Dream in
  Everyday English
- Midsummer Night's Dream
  Questions & Answers
- Much Ado About Nothing
- Othello
- Othello – Questions & Answers
- Richard II
- Richard III
- Romeo and Juliet
- Romeo and Juliet
  in Everyday English
- Romeo and Juliet
  Questions & Answers
- Taming of the Shrew
- Tempest
- Twelfth Night

SHAKESPEARE TSE*

- Hamlet T.S.E.
- Julius Caesar T.S.E.
- King Henry IV – Part I T.S.E.
- King Lear T.S.E.
- Macbeth T.S.E.
- Merchant of Venice T.S.E.
- Othello T.S.E.
- Romeo and Juliet T.S.E.
- Taming of the Shrew T.S.E.
- Tempest T.S.E.
- Twelfth Night T.S.E.

*Total Study Edition

LITERATURE AND POETRY

- Animal Farm
- Brave New World
- Catch 22
- Catcher in the Rye, Nine Stories
- Chrysalids, Day of the Triffids
- Crucible
- Death of a Salesman
- Diviners
- Duddy Kravitz and Other Works
- Edible Woman
- Emma
- Fahrenheit 451
- Farewell to Arms
- Fifth Business
- Glass Menagerie
- Grapes of Wrath
- Great Expectations
- Great Gatsby
- Gulliver's Travels
- Heart of Darkness
- Huckleberry Finn
- Iliad
- Jane Eyre
- King Oedipus, Oedipus at Colonus
- Lord of the Flies
- Lord of the Rings, Hobbit
- Man for All Seasons
- Mayor of Casterbridge
- 1984
- Odyssey
- Of Mice and Men
- Old Man and the Sea
- One Flew Over the Cuckoos Nest
- Paradise Lost
- Pride and Prejudice
- Machiavelli's The Prince
- Scarlet Letter
- Separate Peace
- Stone Angel and Other Works
- Street Car Named Desire
- Surfacing
- Tale of Two Cities
- Tess of the D'Urbervilles
- To Kill a Mockingbird
- Two Solitudes
- Who Has Seen the Wind
- Wuthering Heights

THE CANTERBURY TALES

- The Canterbury Tales
- Prologue to the Canterbury Tales
  Total Study Edition
- Prologue to the Canterbury Tales
- French Verbs Simplified

HOW TO GET AN A IN ...

- Calculus
- Permutations, Combinations &
  Probability
- School Projects & Presentations
- Senior Algebra
- Senior English Essays
- Senior Physics
- Sequences & Series
- Statistics & Data Analysis
- Trigonometry & Circle Geometry

BIOLOGY

- Biology Notes

CHEMISTRY

- Elementary Chemistry Notes Rev.
- How to Solve Chemistry Problems
- Introduction to Chemistry
- Senior Chemistry Notes Rev.

MATHEMATICS

- Elementary Algebra Notes
- Secondary School Mathematics 1
- Secondary School Mathematics 4

PHYSICS

- Elementary Physics Notes
- Senior Physics

REFERENCE

- Dictionary of Literary Terms
- Effective Term Papers and Reports
- English Grammar Simplified
- Handbook of English Grammar &
  Composition
- How to Write Good Essays & Critical
  Reviews
- Secrets of Studying English

For fifty years, Coles Notes have been helping
students get through high school and university.
New Coles Notes will help get you through the rest of life.

Look for these NEW COLES NOTES!

BUSINESS

- Effective Business Presentations
- Accounting for Small Business
- Write Effective Business Letters
- Write a Great Résumé
- Do A Great Job Interview
- Start Your Own Small Business
- Get Ahead at Work

GARDENING

- Indoor Gardening
- Perennial Gardening
- Herb Gardening
- Organic Gardening

LIFESTYLE

- Wine
- Bartending
- Wedding
- Opera
- Casino Gambling
- Better Bridge
- Better Chess
- Better Tennis
- Better Golf
- Public Speaking
- Speed Reading
- Cooking 101
- Scholarships and Bursaries
- Cats and Cat Care
- Dog and Dog Care

PARENTING

- Your Child: The First Year
- Your Child: The Terrific Twos
- Your Child: Ages Three and Four
- Raising A Reader
- Helping Your Child in Math

PERSONAL FINANCE

- Basic Investing
- Investing in Stocks
- Investing in Mutual Funds
- Buying and Selling Your Home
- Plan Your Estate
- Develop a Personal Financial Plan

PHRASE BOOKS

- French
- Spanish
- Italian
- German
- Russian
- Japanese
- Greek

SPORTS FOR KIDS

- Basketball for Kids
- Baseball for Kids
- Soccer for Kids
- Hockey for Kids
- Gymnastics for Kids
- Martial Arts for Kids

Coles Notes and New Coles Notes are available at the following stores:
Chapters • Coles • Smithbooks • World's Biggest Bookstore

NOTES & UPDATES

NOTES & UPDATES